Magical Unicorn Christmas Activity Book

ARCTURUS

ARCTURUS

This edition published in 2018 by Arcturus Publishing Limited
26/27 Bickels Yard, 151–153 Bermondsey Street,
London SE1 3HA

ISBN: 978-1-78888-154-8
CH006436NT
Supplier 29, Date 0718, Print run 6986

Author: Sam Noonan
Illustrator: Sam Loman
Editor: Susannah Bailey
Designer: Well Nice Ltd

Printed in China

Decoration Doodle

It's Christmas time in Unicorn Land and Stardust has started decorating her Christmas tree. Draw some magical decorations to help her finish it.

SNOW SHADOWS

Rainbow and Twinkle have built a snow unicorn!
Can you see which shadow matches it exactly?

Friend Finder

Sparkle is writing her Christmas card list, and doesn't want to miss anybody out.
Can you help her find all her friends' names in the grid below?

STARDUST   SHIMMY   ~~RAINBOW~~   ~~TWINKLE~~

SNOWY   GLITTER   ~~MISTY~~   ~~MUFF~~

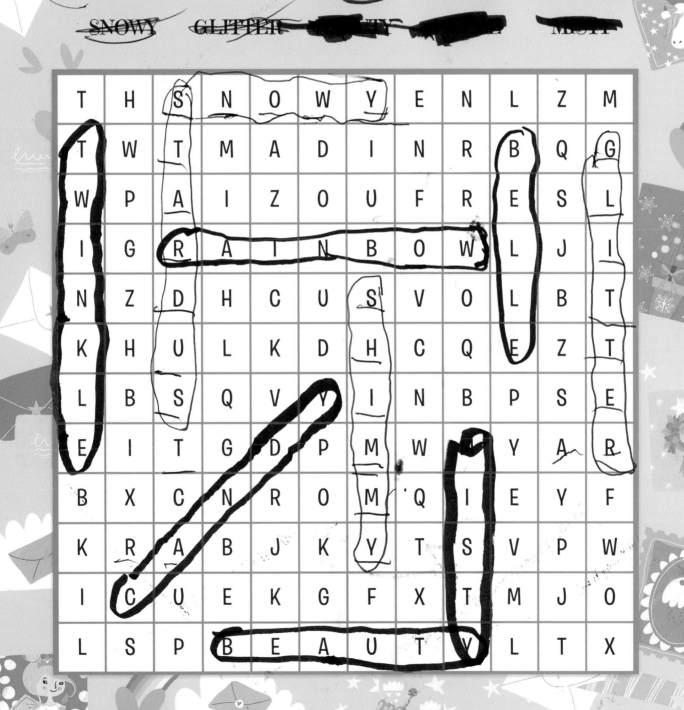

T	H	S	N	O	W	Y	E	N	L	Z	M
T	W	T	M	A	D	I	N	R	B	Q	G
W	P	A	I	Z	O	U	F	R	E	S	L
I	G	R	A	I	N	B	O	W	L	J	I
N	Z	D	H	C	U	S	V	O	L	B	T
K	H	U	L	K	D	H	C	Q	E	Z	T
L	B	S	Q	V	Y	I	N	B	P	S	E
E	I	T	G	D	P	M	W	Y	A	R
B	X	C	N	R	O	M	Q	I	E	Y	F
K	R	A	B	J	K	Y	T	S	V	P	W
I	C	U	E	K	G	F	X	T	M	J	O
L	S	P	B	E	A	U	T	V	L	T	X

Creative Cards

Misty loves making her own Christmas cards to send to her family and friends. Have a go at drawing your own Christmas card design, then write a nice message inside.

To Santa

I Know Christmas has past

but I want something for

all of us So my wish is for

evrybody to have good luck

this year.

Dazzling Decorations

Rainbow wants to buy as many beautiful decorations as she can. She has 17 gold coins to spend. If she buys a star for her tree, how many baubles can she afford?

stars: 5
gold coins

Baubles: 3
gold coins

Festive Lights!

Shimmy, Belle, and Twinkle have taken a trip into the Magic Village to look at the Christmas lights. They love how pretty it all is! Take a good look at the scene and then turn the page to answer some questions from memory.

Belle

Shimmy

Twinkle

Festive Lights! (continued)

See if you can answer these questions without peeking back.

1. Is Belle wearing a pink or purple scarf?

   pink
   ----

2. How many streetlights are in the picture?

   ----

3. Shimmy is looking in a store window. What does the store sell? --------------------------

4. True or false: There is a cat in the picture.

   ----

5. Twinkle is carrying a shopping bag. What has she bought? --------------------------

6. Who or what is flying? --------------------------

Tinsel Tangle

The unicorns are decorating their Christmas trees, but their tinsel has become tangled! Can you work out which unicorn is decorating which tree?

A

B

C

1

2

3

Secret List

Merry loves making presents for her family and friends. Try writing a list of nice things you could make for all your loved ones at Christmas.

1

2

3

4

5

ODD COOKIE

Candy has baked some Christmas gingerbread men, but one doesn't match! Can you tell which one it is?

1

2

3

4

5

6

Magic Market

The unicorns are having fun at the
Cloudpark Christmas Market!
Fill in this magical scene.

Which Wands?

The unicorns' fairy friends cast lots of spells at Christmas time, to make it as magical as possible. Can you find this exact sequence of wands in the grid below?

Hungry Hunt

Sweetie Pie is baking Christmas treats for her friends, but her ingredients have gone missing! Can you find them?

- 3 unbroken eggs
- 2 pairs of cherries
- 1 pat of butter
- 1 jar of sprinkles

16

YOU-NICORN!

What would your unicorn name be? Take the first letter of your name to find out!
You can see what your friends' names would be too.

A: Glitter

B: Twinkle

C: Merry

D: Snowy

E: Giggle

F: Icy

G: Dazzle

H: Sparkle

I: Happy

J: Pretty

K: Misty

L: Sweet

M: Beauty

N: Jolly

O: Moon

P: Charming

Q: Dainty

R: Shimmy

S: Glimmer

T: Flicker

U: Golden

V: Beauty

W: Holly

X: Starry

Y: Glow

Z: Sunny

MY NAME WOULD BE:

MY BEST FRIEND'S NAME WOULD BE:

Misty's Muddle!

Misty has wrapped presents for all of her friends, but she forgot to put labels on them! She's trying to find Stardust's gift.
Can you solve the clues below to find out which one it is?

1. It isn't stripy.

2. It isn't the smallest one.

3. It has a bow.

4. The wrapping paper doesn't have a pattern.

A

B

C

D

E

MOUNTAIN MAZE

Stardust wants to ski through the snow to her present in the middle.
Can you help her find the way?

Start

Finish

Twinkle Toes

All the unicorns wear their best sparkly horseshoes at Christmas!
Beauty has lots, but they're in a muddle. Can you help match up all the pairs?

Work of Art

Twins Shimmy and Shiny love making snow unicorns at Christmas time.
Can you spot eight differences between this year's photo and the last?

Peeking In

Glitter has said nobody can come in while she wraps presents, but her naughty little sisters are peeking! Can you tell which jigsaw pieces complete the scene?

A

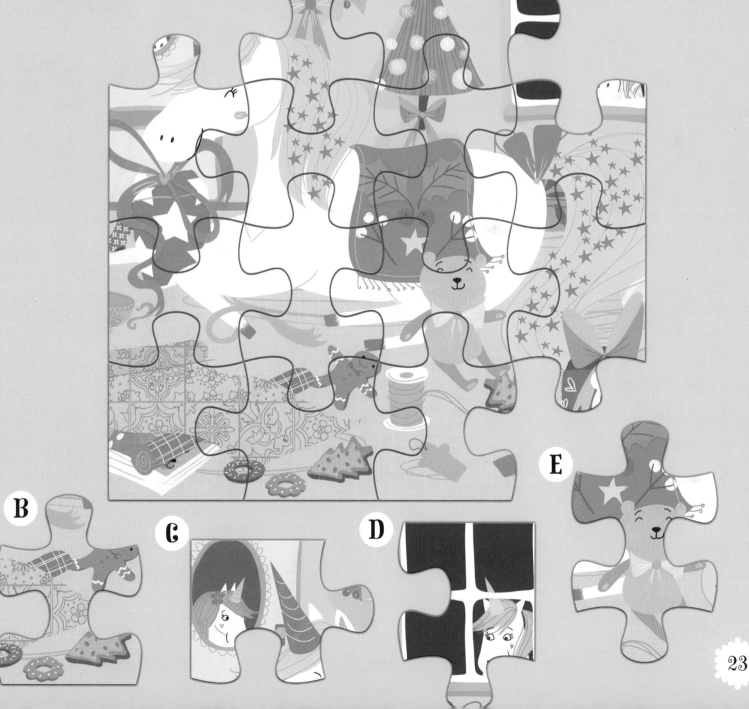

B

C

D

E

Sunny's Smoothies

It isn't winter everywhere: Sunny and her friends celebrate Christmas at the beach! Sunny has made fruity drinks to cool everyone down. Can you spot the odd one out?

A   B   C   D

Christmas Clues

Belle has made Dreamy a Christmas treasure hunt! Help her follow the sprigs of holly to the special Christmas present. She can move up, down, left, and right, but not diagonally.

Start

Finish

Festive Fashion!

Everyone loves fun Christmas sweaters, especially the elves.
Decorate your own Christmas sweater, and be as creative as you like!

Toy Total

The Christmas fairies are packing up toys!
How many cute teddy bears can you count?

Game Time!

Oh no! Misty and Sparkle have spilled all the playing pieces from their board game. The pieces come in pairs, except for one. Can you find the odd one out?

Singalong

At this time of year, the unicorns sing special Christmas songs together. Try making up one of your own. Here are some words to help you start:

Love

Candle

Presents

Snow

Hug

Holly

Tree

Glow

Drinks Order

Sparkle is the best at making delicious drinks in her coffee shop. Can you find these drinks in this exact order (from left to right) in the grid below?

Shining Bright!

Rainbow is very proud of her Christmas lights display.
Complete it, to make it look extra special.

Peaceful Dreams

Baby Gem is snuggling down in bed.
Can you spot eight differences between these sleepy scenes?

Countdown!

Twinkle loves all of the yummy treats around at this time of year! Count the number of gingerbread men, and the number of snowflake cookies. Add them up to see how many days are left until Christmas!

_ _ _	Gingerbread men	_ _ _	Snowflake cookies	_ _ _	Days until Christmas

Great Skates

The magic lake has completely frozen over, and everyone is out ice skating! Can you find these things hidden in the scene?

An owl

A snow mouse

3 lost mittens

An ice-skating fairy

2 pairs of green earmuffs

5 pine trees

34

Christmas Clothes

All the unicorns and their friends love getting dressed up in their special Christmas outfits. Draw an outfit you would love to wear on Christmas Day.

Pretty Mane

Candy loves to put sparkly hair clips in her mane when she goes to Christmas parties. Can you tell which type of hair clips is the one she likes best? Count them and see!

PERFECT PARTY!

It's Stardust's Christmas party! Ten baby fairies have sneaked out of bed to join in the fun. Can you spot them all?

Fir Forest

Misty and Belle are looking for the perfect Christmas tree. Solve the problems below, then add up the answers to find out which tree they should pick.

5 + 6 =

17 - 15 =

5 x 2 =

11 - 4 =

35

44

25

50

12

30

Special Stars

The unicorns love to go stargazing, and spot all the shapes in the sky over Unicorn Land. Look carefully at this scene, then turn the page, and answer some questions from memory.

Special Stars (continued)

See if you can answer these questions without peeking back at the picture.

1. What shape is in the stars on the right of the picture? ....

2. How many shapes are in the stars altogether? ....

3. Which plant is in the stars? ....

4. How many unicorns are stargazing? ....

5. Which little animal has crept out to watch the stars? ....

6. How many fairies are there? ....

Gorgeous Gifts

The best thing about Christmas is giving presents to family and friends.
Can you find all the gifts the unicorns are giving this year?

SHOES SCARF TEDDY NECKLACE
COMB BOOK BLANKET PERFUME

I	C	W	N	S	V	R	K	N	N	D	A
G	B	J	Q	L	H	S	Y	B	E	G	R
T	S	Z	P	X	I	O	C	F	C	P	J
E	B	M	J	S	A	B	E	T	K	W	P
D	G	D	R	C	Q	S	E	S	L	S	K
D	Q	C	K	A	E	M	R	V	A	K	O
Y	N	X	F	R	U	J	C	D	C	H	O
T	K	F	T	F	Y	L	V	S	E	Z	B
X	W	P	R	W	E	C	O	M	B	E	U
M	H	E	Q	E	D	R	D	X	U	M	I
H	P	Z	L	O	B	L	A	N	K	E	T
L	H	Y	E	J	V	M	N	F	G	O	L

Christmas Creations

All of the Christmas unicorns have different types of magic. Look at the examples below, then draw and name your own Christmas unicorns!

1

Candy can make anything taste delicious! She loves making yummy treats for all her unicorn friends. Rainbow says that Candy even makes sprouts taste good!

2

Snowy can make snow fall, and turn water into ice. She makes sure Unicorn Land is covered in pretty snow in time for Christmas!

This is ....

Her power is ....

This is ....

Her power is ....

Paper Patterns

Design your own Christmas wrapping paper. You can draw a repeating pattern, or simply doodle and let your imagination flow!

DAINTY DECORATIONS

Look at all these bright Christmas decorations.
Can you find the only matching pair?

A Festive Fall

Snowy is using her magic to make fresh snowfall for Christmas!
Can you tell which jigsaw piece completes the scene?

Frosty Snowflakes

Snow has now swept through Magic Land! Can you find a way back to the houses, following only the special snowflake? You can move up, down, left, and right, but not diagonally.

Start

Finish

All Bundled Up!

Candy and Shimmy are ready to go on a wintry walk.
Can you copy the picture of them onto the grid below?

Christmas Trinkets

Rainbow loves setting out her Christmas ornaments in a particular order. Can you find this exact sequence (from left to right) in the grid below?

Fairy Frolics

It's the fairy Christmas ballet!
Fill in and decorate this scene.

Cooking for Christmas

Glitter is getting ready to cook everybody a lovely Christmas Eve dinner. She's got all the traditional unicorn treats—sparkle soup, candy crispies, rainbow puffs, and cloud cream! Write your own magical menu for a special Christmas Eve dinner with your friends.

STARTER

....

MAIN

....

DESSERT

....

DRINKS

....

Seasonal Songs

All the unicorns, elves, and fairies love singing Christmas
carols and playing their instruments together.
Can you find these instruments in the grid below?

FLUTE	CLARINET	PIANO	ORGAN	GUITAR
TRUMPET	DRUM	VIOLIN	TRIANGLE	OBOE

H	R	Y	W	M	J	R	I	O	B	O	E
P	P	C	H	N	P	D	F	R	T	G	C
G	U	I	T	A	R	Q	H	G	S	S	L
T	D	V	A	W	P	X	V	A	C	Y	A
R	H	G	Z	N	L	F	G	N	D	F	R
U	T	Y	X	P	O	D	S	J	R	V	I
M	T	R	I	A	N	G	L	E	M	I	N
P	S	T	Y	C	Z	E	Q	T	V	O	E
E	N	F	M	R	L	T	J	B	Z	L	T
T	W	U	J	S	X	U	K	Y	Q	I	K
O	R	E	L	C	Q	L	K	W	B	N	V
D	N	B	M	Z	N	F	D	G	L	M	L

Wrapping Tangle

These unicorns were all wrapping presents, but their pretty ribbons are now all tangled up! Can you sort them out again to figure out who was wrapping each one?

Festive Flowers

Stardust has made some beautiful Christmas wreaths!
Can you find the one that looks a little bit different?

Rainbow Rush

It's rainbow sledging time!
Can you untangle the twisted routes to
find out who won the race?

1

2

3

1st

2nd

3rd

Charade Shadow

Dreamy looks so funny playing charades at the Christmas Games night!
Can you find a shadow that matches her exactly?

Sock Swap

Cloudy knitted magical warming socks for her
elf friends, but now they're all jumbled up!
Can you match the finished ones back into pairs?

Magic Address Book

All the unicorns live in magical places.
Look at the cute unicorn addresses on this page, and
then try making up a magical address of your own!

Beauty,
Perfect Cottage,
Smiling Lane

Candy
Candlebright House,
Star Street

Twinkle
Chocolate Cottage,
Yummy Hill

Christmas Picnic!

It's pretty outside in the snow, so the unicorns are having
a big Christmas feast! Fill in this fun scene.

63

FLYING SNOWBALLS

The elves and fairies are having a big snowball fight!
Can you work out which jigsaw pieces go where, to complete the scene?

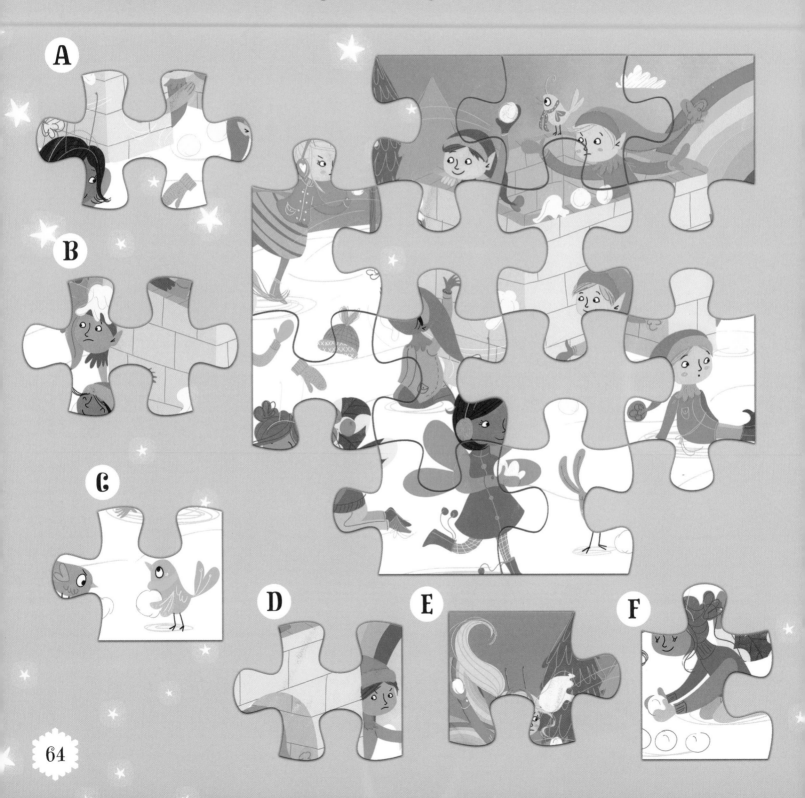

Special Delivery!

Glitter is helping Fern, the elf, deliver presents. Can you help Glitter follow Fern's footsteps through the grid? She can only move up, down, left, and right, not diagonally.

= Fern's Steps

Finish

Start

Party Time

Belle loves Christmas because there are so many fun parties!
This is the Christmas party look she likes best.
Can you recreate it in the grid?

Snowdrift Struggle

Stardust and Twinkle are on their way to a Christmas party. Can you help them find their way?

Start

Finish

GOT TO GIVE

What kind of Christmas gift giver are you? Do the quiz below to find out.

1. If I had a big box of cookies to share with my friends, I would...

   a. give them all away and not take any for myself.
   b. put a nice little note with each one, to make my friends smile.
   c. send my friends on a fun treasure hunt to find the cookies!

2. When I go to a party, I...

   a. always take a gift with me.
   b. arrive early to help set up.
   c. try to talk to everyone!

3. The best thing about Christmas is...

   a. giving presents, of course!
   b. spending time with my family and friends.
   c. playing silly games together.

4. The best Christmas sweater is...

   a. the one that matches with the one I got for my friend.
   b. the one that was a special gift.
   c. the one that lights up and plays tunes!

5. The best Christmas song is...

a. the one my family likes best.
b. the one that has the best lyrics.
c. the one that makes you want to dance.

6. The best Christmas outfit is...

a. one that someone has given you.
b. something interesting and unusual.
c. something bright and eye-catching.

MOSTLY As

GENEROUS

You like giving gifts to all of your family and friends, and you don't hold back at Christmas. You just like to spoil everyone!

MOSTLY Bs

THOUGHTFUL

You like to give presents that have a lot of meaning. Perhaps they are things you have made yourself, or that you know mean a lot to the other person. They are always sweet, and touch people's hearts!

MOSTLY Cs

EXCITING

You love to give weird and wonderful presents. The wackier the better! You like to surprise people, and Christmas Day with you is never dull!

Sunset Arrival

The unicorns' reindeer cousins have come to visit!
Complete this magical sunset scene.

Flying Reindeer!

Here comes Jolly the reindeer!
Can you tell which picture of him is the odd one out?

Under the Sea

The Christmas mermaids are having a party.
Can you spot eight differences between the scenes?

Shall We Dance?

It's the Magical Creature Ball! Look carefully at this scene, and then turn the page to answer some questions from memory.

Shall We Dance? (continued)

See if you can answer these questions!

1. How many creatures are wearing purple? ---------------------------

2. Are there drums in the picture? ---------------------------

3. What shape are the Christmas tree decorations? ---------------------------

4. Is anyone wearing a hat? ---------------------------

5. What is the baby fairy doing? ---------------------------

6. How many unicorns are singing? ---------------------------

Bird Buddies

Snowy likes to give Christmas presents to the birds: special nut and seed balls!
Can you spot which little bird is the odd one out?

Workshop Whirl!

The Christmas elves are rushing to finish off all the presents in time!
Can you spot the three items below in the main picture?

A doll with pigtails

A unicorn toy

A soft rabbit

Bedtime Blues

Fairy Frida has lost her teddy bear. She can't go to sleep on Christmas Eve without it. Which path will help her find it?

A   B   C

Doll

Teddy

Train

FROZEN FLURRY!

All snowflakes are meant to be unique, but Glitter has found a matching pair!
Can you spot them?

Secret Santa

Dreamy has been given a beautiful ribbon in the Secret Santa exchange.
Can you work out who her gift giver is?

1. There is no green on this unicorn.

2. She is not wearing a bow.

3. Her mane has a pattern.

A

Beauty

C

Misty

B

Sweetie Pie

D

Snowy

Winter Woods

Cloudy and Sweetie Pie have found a lost fairy in the wintry woods! Can you guide her home?

Start

Finish

Festive Breakfast

It's time for a Christmassy breakfast. Cute cupcakes all around! Decorate this plate with a Christmas pattern, then add some yummy food to eat.

Sleigh Ride

Father Christmas is letting the unicorns take a turn at pulling his sleigh.
Can you spot eight differences between the two pictures?

FESTIVE FEAST

It's Christmas dinner time, and Candy has invited her friends over to eat.
Can you spot whose plate doesn't have everything?

Jolly Jumble

Sparkle is choosing Christmas decorations for her home. Can you put the scene of her with them back together?

Present Time!

All the friends are opening their presents under the big Christmas tree! Can you find these elements in the scene?

A little elf cuddling his new doll.

A fairy helping tie a unicorn's tail bow.

Two new horseshoes.

Reunicorn!

It's a unicorn family reunion! Grandpa Foggy is here, along with Aunty Moon, and all the unicorn cousins. Can you spot eight differences between the two scenes?

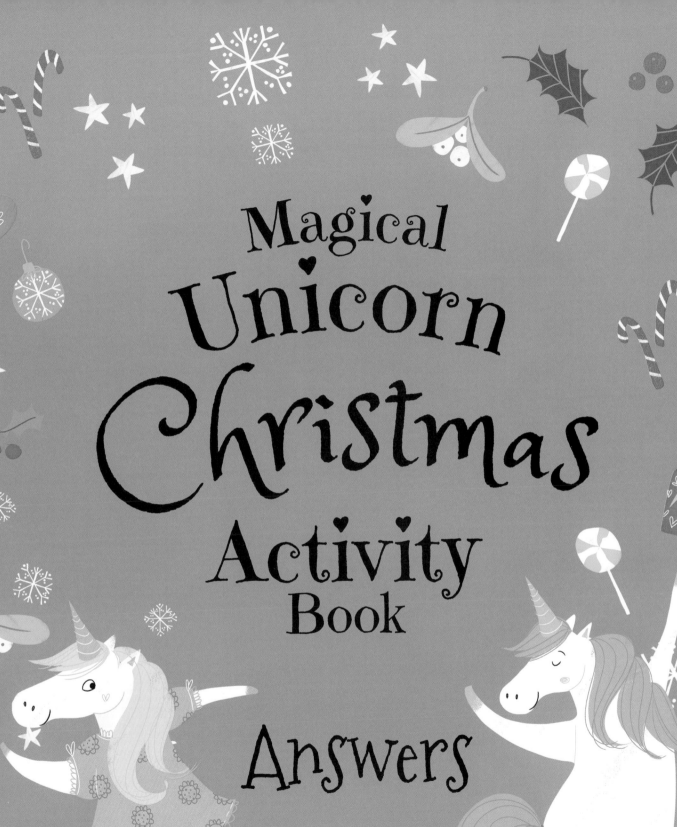

Magical
Unicorn
Christmas
Activity
Book

Answers

Answers

Page 4: Snow Shadows

Page 5: Friend Finder

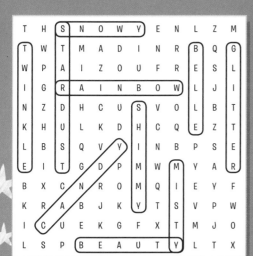

Page 8: Dazzling Decorations

Rainbow can afford 4 baubles.

Page 10: Festive Lights!

1. Purple.
2. 5.
3. Toys.
4. True.
5. Cupcakes.
6. Fairies.

Page 11: Tinsel Tangle

1 - B
2 - C
3 - A

Page 13: Odd Cookie

Page 15: Which Wands?

Answers

Pages 16-17: Hungry Hunt

Page 22: Work of Art

Page 19: Misty's Muddle!

B

Page 20: Mountain Maze

Page 21: Twinkle Toes

Page 23: Peeking In

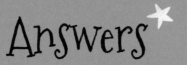

Answers

Page 24: Sunny's Smoothies

Page 27: Toy Total

There are 11 bears.

Page 28: Game Time!

Page 32: Peaceful Dreams

Page 25: Christmas Clues

Page 33: Countdown!

3 gingerbread men + 4 snowflake cookies
= 7 days until Christmas

Page 30: Drinks Order

Answers

Pages 34-35: Great Skates

Page 37: Pretty Mane

Candy likes the star hair clips best.

Pages 38-39: Perfect Party!

Page 40: Fir Forest

5 + 6 = 11

17 - 15 = 2

2 x 5 = 10

11 - 4 = 7

Final answer: 30

Page 42: Special Stars

1. A rainbow.
2. 5.
3. A Christmas tree/fir tree.
4. 4.
5. A mouse.
6. 3.

Page 43: Gorgeous Gifts

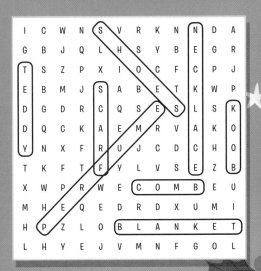

Answers

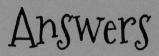

Page 47: Dainty Decorations

Page 49: Frosty Snowflakes

Page 55: Seasonal Songs

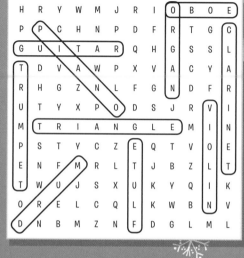

Page 56: Wrapping Tangle

1 C
2 B
3 A

Page 48: A Festive Fall

Page 51: Christmas Trinkets

Page 57: Festive Flowers

Answers

Page 58: Rainbow Rush

1 3rd
2 2nd
3 1st

Page 59: Charade Shadow

Page 60: Sock Swap

Page 64: Flying Snowballs

Page 65: Special Delivery

Page 67: Snowdrift Struggle

Page 71: Flying Reindeer!

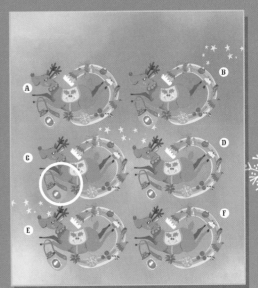

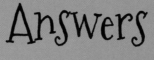

Answers

Page 72: Under the Sea

Page 75: Bird Buddies

Page 77: Bedtime Blues

A. Train
B. Teddy
C. Doll

Page 78: Frozen Flurry!

Page 74: Shall We Dance?

1. 4.
2. Yes.
3. Stars.
4. Yes.
5. Decorating the tree.
6. 1.

Page 76: Workshop Whirl!

Page 79: Secret Santa

D

Answers

Page 80: Winter Woods

Page 83: Festive Feast

Page 85: Present Time!

Page 82: Sleigh Ride

Page 84: Jolly Jumble

Page 86: Reunicorn!

Have a magical Christmas!